Together in Prayer
Intercessions based on biblical themes

Book 2

Susan Sayers

Kevin
Mayhew

This edition published in 1999 by
KEVIN MAYHEW LTD
Buxhall
Stowmarket
Suffolk IP14 3DJ

These intercessions first appeared in
Living Stones – Complete Resource Book

Unless indicated otherwise, Scripture quotations are taken from
New Revised Standard Version Bible, copyright © 1989, by the
Division of Christian Education of the National Council of the
Churches of Christ in the United States of America.

ISBN 1 84003 346 0
Catalogue No 1 500265

Cover design by Jaquetta Sergeant
Edited by Peter Dainty
Typesetting by Richard Weaver
Printed and bound in Great Britain

Foreword

A praying church is a living organism, powered by the love of God, and directed by his will. The aim of those leading intercessions in public worship is to provide a suitable climate for prayer, both for the faithful core of praying members, and also for those who drift in as visitors, sometimes willingly and sometimes rather grudgingly.

Since our God is in a far better position to know the needs of each muddle of people who arrive on any particular Sunday, it is obviously sensible to prepare for leading the intercessions by praying for those who will be there, asking our God to lead us with his agenda in mind, rather than taking immediate charge ourselves. Then we have to give him a chance to answer! You may find that a quiet walk enables you to do this, or a time wandering round the empty church, or time spent on some of the mechanical jobs at home while you still your heart and resist the temptation to badger God with good ideas.

The ideas I have provided here may well spark off other thoughts of your own. Do use them however you wish – exactly as they stand, adapted to suit specific needs, or simply as a starting point. They are a resource to help you, not a cage to imprison you.

During the service be alert to what is being said and how God is moving among you, so that you can pick up on these threads, if it seems appropriate, during the intercessions. And if you have young children present, give some thought to how they can also be praying at this time. They might be following a picture prayer trail, singing a quiet worship song, drawing some situation they are praying for, or looking through the intercession pictures provided in children's communion books, such as *Jesus is Here* (Kevin Mayhew, 1993).

I have heard it said that since God can hear the prayers, it doesn't really matter if the congregation can't.

I don't agree. In public worship it can be very distracting to be straining to hear, or isolating if you can hear only a vague mumble. Do take the trouble to practise speaking clearly and fairly slowly in the church, so that everyone can comfortably take in what you are saying. Bear in mind that nerves usually make us speed up somewhat, so speak extra slowly to allow for this.

Finally, don't recite what you have written, but pray it. Pray it both through the intentions and through the silences. Leading the intercessions carries a great responsibility, but it is also a great privilege.

SUSAN SAYERS

Contents

—OUR HEAVENLY FATHER—

God of Heaven

Our Father in heaven
Matthew 6:9

Let us pray to the great God of heaven
who stands among us now.

Heavenly God, as the earthly part of your Church
we come before you with our thanks and praise
for your living presence among us,
in our worship together
and in our separate times of prayer.
We thank you for bringing the joy of heaven to earth
as you lift us into your presence.

Silence

You are our God:
living for ever and ever.

Look with mercy on our world
as we work out policies and target needs,
and misunderstand one another's cultures
and get carried away with excesses
and the taste of power.

Silence

You are our God:
living for ever and ever.

May our waking, working, eating, relaxing and sleeping
become a pattern coloured and lit by your love;
may our homes reflect it,
our places of work be energised by it,
and our relationships glow with it.

Silence

You are our God:
living for ever and ever.

To those who are losing heart
give your heavenly encouragement and patience;
to the young and vulnerable
give heavenly protection;
to the ill and the damaged
give heavenly healing and inner peace,
as you touch our lives with yours.

Silence

You are our God:
living for ever and ever.

Knowing that physical death
is not the end of life,
but the beginning of a new dimension,
we recall our loved ones who have died
and commend them to your eternal keeping.

Silence

You are our God:
living for ever and ever.

As you fill our hearts with heavenly joy
we pour out our love and praise
to you, our living God!

Merciful Father,
accept these prayers
for the sake of your Son,
our Saviour Jesus Christ. Amen.

Lord of Creation

In the beginning God created the heavens and the earth.
Genesis 1:1 (NIV)

Humankind has been brought into life by God.
We owe our very existence to him.
Let us pray to him now.

We pray for each living person
inhabiting our world with us,
with all the needs, emotions and experiences we share.
We pray that we may recognise one another
as brothers and sisters
sharing the same heavenly Father.

Silence

Lord of creation:
let your will be done.

We pray for greater reverence for God's creation
in the way we use and manage resources and wildlife.

Silence

Lord of creation:
let your will be done.

We pray for all of us in the ship of the Church,
that whenever storms rock the boat
and appear to threaten us,
we may trust God to bring us safely through.

Silence

Lord of creation:
let your will be done.

We pray for our children
and for all giving birth and being born today.
We long for the world they enter to be welcoming
and full of God's practical love.

Silence

Lord of creation:
let your will be done.

We pray for those who have chronic illness
and have to live in constant pain.
We ask for God's comfort
and reassurance to support them.

Silence

Lord of creation:
let your will be done.

We pray for those who have died,
thanking God for the example of lives well lived,
and for the total healing now received.

Merciful Father,
**accept these prayers
for the sake of your Son,
our Saviour Jesus Christ. Amen.**

The Ground of Our Being

In him we live and move and have our being.
Acts 17:28

Let us focus our gaze on the great God who made us,
as we pour out to him our prayers.

Lord of all, give your Church such maturity and wisdom
that we may not be swayed from our purpose and calling
by trivialities or worldly pressures,
but know increasingly our dependence
on you in all things and proclaim your Gospel
with steadfastness and joy.

Silence

You, O Lord:
are the ground of our being.

Lord of all, give to all leaders
and heads of state graciousness and integrity,
that all in power and authority
may undertake their duties in a spirit of humility;
that the oppressed may find a voice,
and the nations work together for the good of the world.

Silence

You, O Lord:
are the ground of our being.

Lord of all, give to our homes
and places of work and leisure your harmony and peace;
give us grace to respect one another and ourselves
in the way we talk and think, and in the way we behave.

Silence

You, O Lord:
are the ground of our being.

Lord of all, speak your peace into the hearts
of all who are agitated, anxious or confused.
Lay your hands of healing on all who are ill
and let them know your reassurance and love.

Silence

You, O Lord:
are the ground of our being.

Lord of all, welcome into your kingdom
all who have kept faith
and now can lay their burdens down.
May they rest in your peace for ever.

Silence

You, O Lord:
are the ground of our being.

Lord of all, the order and complexity of creation
sings your praise,
and we give voice to it now
as we offer you our song of lives rededicated
to the work of your kingdom.

Merciful Father,
**accept these prayers
for the sake of your Son,
our Saviour Jesus Christ. Amen.**

Ever-faithful God

The faithfulness of the Lord endures for ever.
Psalm 117:2

Loving God, because we trust you,
we come to you now with our concerns
for the Church and the world.

We bring all those who find it so hard to believe,
so hard to trust in a faithful loving God;
we bring those who teach the faith;
all who preach and chat the good news.
Give the right words for each situation and each person,
and enable the seed to take root and grow.

Silence   Ever-faithful God:
         in you we put our trust.

We bring those whose authority and decisions
affect the lives of many people and the health of the
    planet.
We pray for sensitivity and honesty,
and the strength to retain integrity
even in positions of power.

Silence   Ever-faithful God:
         in you we put our trust.

We bring the newly born and their parents,
and all whose family circumstances face change;
give us the spiritual flexibility
to adapt to your guiding in all our relationships,
and above all in our relationship with you.

Silence   Ever-faithful God:
                                  in you we put our trust.

We bring all for whom illness or injury
has caused disruption, uncertainty
and the prospect of long-term change;
all who find their lives are spinning
out of their control;
give them working knowledge
of your total loving and unchanging presence,
so that in all the changes and troubles of life
they may be assured of your everlasting protection.

Silence   Ever-faithful God:
                                  in you we put our trust.

We commend to your love and mercy
all those who have made the journey through death,
especially any who have died unprepared,
or violent deaths.
We thank you for your understanding and compassion
and pray that they may know the forgiveness,
peace and joy of heaven.

Silence   Ever-faithful God:
                                  in you we put our trust.

As we call to mind the guidance and help
you give us each moment of every day,
we thank you and praise you, Holy God,
for you alone have the words of eternal life.

Merciful Father,
accept these prayers
for the sake of your Son,
our Saviour Jesus Christ. Amen.

God our Companion

The Lord your God is with you wherever you go.
Joshua 1:9

Let us pray to the faithful God who knows us already,
and loves us so much.

We pray that any barriers within the Church,
built up by fear or prejudice, misunderstanding or hurt,
may be broken down in Christ and unity restored.

Silence

As we journey, O Lord:
walk with us on the way.

We pray for our world to be governed wisely and well,
with proper consideration
for the vulnerable and weak,
with co-operation, honesty and respect for all.

Silence

As we journey, O Lord:
walk with us on the way.

We pray for the healing
of hurts and tensions in our families;
and for our friends,
thanking you for the blessings they give;
as friends of Christ, may we be
generous in our friendships.

Silence

As we journey, O Lord:
walk with us on the way.

We pray for those disturbed by mental illness,
and for all who are rejected and despised.
We pray for all in desolate situations at the moment,
and ask for your comfort and healing.

Silence

As we journey, O Lord:
walk with us on the way.

We remember those whose earthly life has ended,
and for those grieving for loved ones.
Enfold them in your love
and let them become aware of you beside them.

Silence

As we journey, O Lord:
walk with us on the way.

We give you thanks, O Lord,
for the loving way you provide for us,
even during the darkest times.

Merciful Father,
**accept these prayers
for the sake of your Son,
our Saviour Jesus Christ. Amen.**

The Everlasting Rock

Trust in the Lord forever, for in the Lord God you have
an everlasting rock.
Isaiah 26:4

As living stones,
let us pray for the building up of God's Church,
and for the world God loves.

Living God, our life is in your hands,
and we offer you all that we are,
all that our past has made us, and all that we may
    become.
Build us up by the power of your Spirit
into a spiritual temple
where you are glorified day after day,
in all our praise and worship,
and in our love for one another.

Silence   You are our strong rock:
                    our strong rock and our shelter.

Living God, our planet,
with its frenzied life on its fragile skin,
is unnervingly small and vulnerable to evil.
Sharpen our consciences to sense your direction
and protect us from all that draws us away from you.
Guide our leaders in the way of truth
and realign us all to the values which are built on you.

Silence   You are our strong rock:
                    our strong rock and our shelter.

Living God, may the Way which Jesus shows us
be the Way we live out our daily lives
around the table, in the daylight and the dark,
in the misunderstandings, the tensions and the rush,
in the eye contact, the conversations and the growing.

Silence   You are our strong rock:
                    our strong rock and our shelter.

Living God,
we pray for all who feel out of their depth,
who are drowning in their pain, sorrow and guilt.
Save them, Lord,
and help them to a place of safety.
Fix their feet on the solid rock of your love.

Silence   You are our strong rock:
                    our strong rock and our shelter.

Living God, we remember those who have died
and pray for them now.
Lead them out of their pain
into the light of eternity,
and keep us all in the Way that leads us
to share that everlasting life with you.

Silence   You are our strong rock:
                    our strong rock and our shelter.

Living God, we thank you
for showing us the Way,
in human terms that we find easier to understand.

Merciful Father,
accept these prayers
for the sake of your Son,
our Saviour Jesus Christ. Amen.

GOD'S WAY

The Way of Love

And I will show you a still more excellent way.
I Corinthians 12:31

Let us bring to the God who loves us
our prayers and concerns for the Church and the world.

God of compassion,
take our hearts of stone
and give us feeling hearts,
so that we as the Church
may be more responsive
to the needs and sorrows around us.

Silence

God of love:
show us the Way.

God of wisdom,
teach all in authority,
inspire those who lead,
protect each nation from evil,
and further each right decision.

Silence

God of love:
show us the Way.

God of tenderness,
dwell in our homes
through all the times of joy

and all the heartaches and sadness,
teaching us to show one another
the love you show to us.

Silence

God of love:
show us the Way.

God of wholeness,
speak into the despair and loneliness
of all who struggle with life and its troubles;
reassure, affirm and encourage them,
and alert us to ways we can help.

Silence

God of love:
show us the Way.

God of peace,
be with the dying,
and as you welcome those who have died in faith
into the full life of your kingdom,
we, too, remember them with thanks and love.

Merciful Father,
**accept these prayers
for the sake of your Son,
our Saviour Jesus Christ. Amen.**

Let Love Increase

And this is my prayer, that your love may overflow
more and more.
Philippians 1:9

As members together of the body of Christ,
let us pray to the true and living God.

We pray for the nurture
of each member of the Church;
for the newly baptised and for all
in ordained and lay ministry,
that our love for one another may show
as we work for the coming of the kingdom.

Silence   Direct our hearts, O Lord:
            to love you more and more.

We pray for the gift of discernment,
so that we recognise God's presence,
and reverence his face
in the faces of those we meet.

Silence   Direct our hearts, O Lord:
            to love you more and more.

We hold before you our monarchy
and all those who govern our country
and make its laws,
that we may act responsibly and with compassion,
attentive to real needs and good values.

Silence   Direct our hearts, O Lord:
            to love you more and more.

We pray particularly for homes
filled with suspicion and envy,
and ask for the healing of old hurts,
together with hope and perseverance
as people set out on paths of reconciliation.

Silence   Direct our hearts, O Lord:
to love you more and more.

We pray for those whose capacity for trust and love
has been damaged by other people's sin.
We long for your healing
so that all who are imprisoned by their past
may walk freely into your future.

Silence   Direct our hearts, O Lord:
to love you more and more.

We pray for those who have recently
passed through death,
that you will judge them with mercy,
so that, made whole in your love,
they may know the joy of your eternity.

Silence   Direct our hearts, O Lord:
to love you more and more.

We give you thanks and praise
for the salvation and restoration
that is now possible for us
through Christ's victory over death.

Merciful Father,
**accept these prayers
for the sake of your Son,
our Saviour Jesus Christ. Amen.**

Your Will Be Done

I delight to do your will, O my God.
Psalm 40:8

Let us pray to God,
knowing we can trust him.

We pray that as Christians we may take to heart
the need to walk the talk,
and live out what we profess.
We pray that nothing may get so important to us
that it pushes God's values aside.

Silence

Father:
let your will be done.

We pray that those in authority and power
do not lose touch with the needs of those they serve,
so that the poor and oppressed and vulnerable
are always given value and respect.

Silence

Father:
let your will be done.

We pray for those in our families
whom we love and have hurt or upset;
we pray too for those who have hurt or upset us,
and ask for God's reconciliation and healing.

Silence

Father:
let your will be done.

We pray for those who have lost hope
of being rescued, noticed or valued;
for the complacent who cannot see their poverty,
for the prejudiced who mistake blindness for sight.

Silence

Father:
let your will be done.

We pray for our loved ones
who have reached the moment of death,
and thank you for the example of their lives.
We commend them all to your safe keeping.

Silence

Father:
let your will be done.

We give you thanks, Lord God, for the hope
and encouragement you give us
on our journey of faith.

Merciful Father,
**accept these prayers
for the sake of your Son,
our Saviour Jesus Christ. Amen.**

Wise Builders

*Everyone who hears these words of mine and acts on
them will be like a wise man who built his house on rock.*
Matthew 7:24

As the community of God's people,
let us focus our attention and still our bodies to pray.

Father, we have heard your words and your challenge
to build our lives wisely on the bedrock of faith;
may all of us who profess to be Christians
act on what we have heard.
Bless and inspire all who preach and teach the faith
and make our worship pure and holy
and acceptable to you.

Silence

Lord God of wisdom:
we build our lives on you.

Father, we are conscious of the double standards
and inconsistencies in our world,
and ask for hearts to be opened to hear you
and recognise the wisdom of your law of love.
We ask you to strengthen and encourage each attempt
to govern with your principles,
and deal justly with your sense of mercy.

Silence

Lord God of wisdom:
we build our lives on you.

Father, we want to take more seriously
our community commitment to our children.

Show us what needs to be started,
developed or changed in our attitudes to one another,
and in the way we help one another's faith to grow.

Silence

Lord God of wisdom:
we build our lives on you.

Father, the needs and concerns of all who suffer
are our concern, through love.
May we strive to address
the imprisoning poverty and hunger
of much of our world,
and involve ourselves in the comfort, help and healing
we ask of you.

Silence

Lord God of wisdom:
we build our lives on you.

Father, we commend to your love and mercy
those who have died to this earthly life.
We thank you for lives well lived and love shared.
Bring them, and us in our turn, safely to heaven.

Silence

Lord God of wisdom:
we build our lives on you.

Father, we thank you that we can stand firm and strong
on the rock of Christ;
build us up in your love and wisdom.

Merciful Father,
accept these prayers
for the sake of your Son,
our Saviour Jesus Christ. Amen.

Justice and Mercy

What doth the Lord require of thee,
but to do justly and to love mercy?
Micah 6:8 (AV)

Let us draw near to the just and merciful God,
and pour out our concerns
for the Church and for the world.

Lord our God,
as we join the unending cycle of prayer on our planet,
turning through time and space,
we rejoice in your upholding, your mercy and forgiveness.
In all our small-mindedness we ask your inbreathing,
so that we learn to look with your vision
and act with your wideness of compassion.

Silence   God of justice and mercy:
                                   hear us as we pray.

Lord our God,
be present at all meetings and negotiations,
where feelings run high,
and many lives are profoundly affected
by the decisions made.
We pray for real communication
which listens to needs and appreciates difficulties,
so that we may live on this earth together
in harmony and peace.

Silence   God of justice and mercy:
                                   hear us as we pray.

Lord our God,
we pray for this neighbourhood

and the particular problems it has;
for communities split apart by conflict
or crushed by tragedy;
we pray for those involved with court proceedings;
may our judicial system uphold your principle
of justice with mercy.

Silence   God of justice and mercy:
                    hear us as we pray.

Lord our God,
we pray for those who have a raw deal in this life;
for those with ongoing health problems,
and all who are caught up in war and deprivation.
We pray for a just and realistic sharing of our resources,
and courage, support and healing for all who suffer.

Silence   God of justice and mercy:
                    hear us as we pray.

Lord our God, we pray for those who have died
and now see their lives as they really are;
we pray for your mercy on them,
and thank you for all their acts of goodness and love.

Silence   God of justice and mercy:
                    hear us as we pray.

Lord our God,
in all the events and phases of our life
we give you thanks
for your steadfast and unchanging love
which sustains and directs us.

Merciful Father,
accept these prayers
for the sake of your Son,
our Saviour Jesus Christ. Amen.

Lead Us, Lord

Lead me in the way everlasting.
Psalm 139:24

God is close to us as we pray.
He is attentive to us now.

Lord, whenever you weep over our harshness,
make your tears melt our hearts of stone.
Whenever you grieve over our double standards,
shock us into honesty again.
Make us receptive to your teaching,
willing to take your risks
and eager to run with our eyes fixed on Jesus.

Silence   Lead us, Lord:
                         to walk in your ways.

Whenever the news overwhelms us,
nudge us to fervent prayer.
Wherever leaders meet to negotiate peace,
be present at the conference table.
Breathe your values into our thinking,
tear down the divisive barriers
and renew us to lead the world into loving.

Silence   Lead us, Lord:
                         to walk in your ways.

Whenever tempers are frayed
and patience is wearing thin,
give us space to collect ourselves and try again.
Whenever the demands of family and friends
remind us of our limitations,

minister graciously through our weakness
and teach us the humility of apologising.

Silence　　　　　　　　Lead us, Lord:
to walk in your ways.

Whenever people are enveloped by pain
or desolate grief or total exhaustion,
bring refreshment and peace, tranquillity and hope.
Wherever the grip of the past
prevents free movement into the future,
bring release and healing.

Silence　　　　　　　　Lead us, Lord:
to walk in your ways.

Whenever the dying are fearful and distressed,
give comfort and reassurance on that last journey.
Bless those who care for them
and those who mourn their going.
In mercy receive the dead
into the life of your heaven,
and prepare us, through our lives now, for eternity.

Silence　　　　　　　　Lead us, Lord:
to walk in your ways.

Holy God, we love the beauty and goodness
of your nature,
and thank you for the gift of your Spirit
to guide us to walk in your ways.

Merciful Father,
accept these prayers
for the sake of your Son,
our Saviour Jesus Christ. Amen.

—OUR LORD JESUS CHRIST—

Emmanuel

*They shall name him Emmanuel, which means
'God is with us'.*
Matthew 1:23

God is here with us now.
Let us pray.

Father, we want to be ready to receive you.
Take us as we are and cultivate in us
a heart that longs for you and worships you
above and beyond everything else.

Silence

Come, O come:
Emmanuel, God with us.

We open to your love
the spiritual journeys of all who walk your way;
protect them from evil
and keep them steadfast in faith.

Silence

Come, O come:
Emmanuel, God with us.

We pray for those who give us support
and encourage us and listen to us
and make us laugh and share our sorrows.
Bless their lives and give them joy.

Silence

Come, O come:
Emmanuel, God with us.

We remember in your presence
those whose memories are painful,
and those whose bitter resentment
cramps and distorts present relationships.
We ask for the healing only God can give.

Silence

Come, O come:
Emmanuel, God with us.

We call to mind those we know who have died,
and any who are close to death at the moment.
As they meet the one true God
open their hearts to receive his love,
mercy and forgiveness.

Silence

Come, O come:
Emmanuel, God with us.

We give God thanks
for the way none of us is beyond his saving love
and the way he has promised
to keep us ultimately safe.

Merciful Father,
**accept these prayers
for the sake of your Son,
our Saviour Jesus Christ. Amen.**

Lord, We Come to You

Anyone who comes to me I will never drive away.
John 6:37

Our loving God is here, attentive to his children.
Let us pray to him now.

Father, we pray that your Church
may always be open to receive your love;
keep us swept clean of pomposity,
complacency or self-righteousness;
let us come humbly and simply into your presence
and wait on you, knowing our dependence on you,
and rejoicing in it.

Silence   As you have called us:
Lord, we come to you.

Father, we pray for all world leaders
and their governments;
for the strength of authority
comes not through force and domination
but through co-operation and mutual respect;
we pray for greater consideration
of the needs of one another and of our planet,
and a desire to right past wrongs and injustices.

Silence   As you have called us:
Lord, we come to you.

Father, we pray for a growing maturity
in our thinking and our loving
that enables us to be childlike;
we pray for healing from all the damage

that prevents us from growing up;
we pray that our children in this church
may be helped to grow strong,
and we thank you for all we learn from them.

Silence   As you have called us:
                                       Lord, we come to you.

Father, we pray for all who cry out for rest and relief,
all who are carrying terrible burdens
that weigh them down,
all whose poverty denies them the chance of healing,
all whose wealth denies them
the chance of knowing their need of you.

Silence   As you have called us:
                                       Lord, we come to you.

Father, we pray for those who die unprepared to meet you,
and for all who have died recently,
both those well-known to us
and those dying unknown and unnoticed
all over the world.

Silence   As you have called us:
                                       Lord, we come to you.

Father, we thank you for your gentleness and humility,
which puts our pride and vanity to shame.
Teach us to trust more and more in your truth,
discarding what the world considers essential
and rejoicing in your freedom.

Merciful Father,
accept these prayers
for the sake of your Son,
our Saviour Jesus Christ. Amen.

Risen with Christ

Consider yourselves dead to sin and alive to God
in Christ Jesus.
Romans 6:11

Let us pray to our heavenly Father,
who is familiar with our world
and understands our humanity.
Lord of all, wherever Christians are ridiculed
or persecuted for their faith,
we ask your courage and inner strength;
wherever we are called to be your witnesses,
we ask for the grace to communicate your love.
Wherever love for you has grown cold
we ask to fan the flames again.

Silence　　　　　　　In Christ we can be dead to sin:
and alive to God.

Lord, wherever the human spirit
is ground down by oppression,
and wherever our silence allows injustice
and corruption to flourish,
we ask for deeper compassion and commitment;
we ask for our kingdoms to become your kingdoms,
and the desires of your heart to be ours.

Silence　　　　　　　In Christ we can be dead to sin:
and alive to God.

Lord of all, wherever families are struggling
to stay together,
and wherever there are ongoing arguments
and family feuds,

we ask your anoint   nquillity and harmony.
Wherever children   nted and unloved,
neglected or in dar   sk your protection and help.

Silence   rist we can be dead to sin:
          alive to God.

Lord, wherever bod   or spirits
are wracked with pa
or too weak or exha   ny,
we ask the bathing l   presence,
and the practical cai   ls working in your name.
Wherever there are c   the battle is strong,
we ask your empowe   ng and clear guidance.

Silence   In Christ we can be dead to sin:
          and alive to God.

Lord of all,
wherever the dying are anxious and afraid,
we ask your peace;
wherever the faithful have passed
from this life into eternity,
we commend them to your unchanging
and everlasting love.

Silence   In Christ we can be dead to sin:
          and alive to God.

Wherever nature's beauty or the daily miracles around us
alert us to see your face, we thank you for the grace
to live this resurrection life.

Merciful Father,
accept these prayers
for the sake of your Son,
our Saviour Jesus Christ. Amen.

Jesus Our King

Blessed is the King who comes in the name of the Lord.
Luke 19:38

Through Jesus, our King, let us pray.

As we celebrate Jesus, the head of the Church body,
we pray for all the members
with their various gifts and ministries;
we pray that even our weaknesses
can be used to your glory
for the good of the world.

Silence

Jesus, our King:
rule in our lives.

May all governments and heads of state
be led in ways of truth and righteousness,
and recognise with humility
that they are called to serve.
We pray for all rescue teams and trouble-shooters;
for all who work to recover the lost.

Silence

Jesus, our King:
rule in our lives.

May we reach out to one another
with greater love and better understanding;
we pray for our homes, our relatives,
our neighbours and our friends,

particularly those who do not yet realise
the extent of your love for them.

Silence

Jesus, our King:
rule in our lives.

May those who have been scattered
far from their homes and loved ones
be enabled to live again in peace and happiness;
may the bitter and resentful find hope again
and the confused find new direction.

Silence

Jesus, our King:
rule in our lives.

May the dying know your closeness,
and those who mourn their loved ones
know for certain that your kingdom
stretches across both sides of death.

Silence

Jesus, our King:
rule in our lives.

Our hearts are filled with thanksgiving
as we realise again
the extraordinary extent of your love for us.

Merciful Father,
**accept these prayers
for the sake of your Son,
our Saviour Jesus Christ. Amen.**

THE HOLY SPIRIT

Come, Holy Spirit

When the Spirit of truth comes, he will guide you
into all the truth.
John 16:13

Let us pray to the God
who calls us each by name.

We pray for all baptised Christians
to live out their calling in loving and holy lives.
We pray for those preparing
for Baptism and Confirmation;
for parents and godparents
to be given the grace and perseverance
to keep faithfully the promises made.

Silence

Come, Holy Spirit:
guide our lives.

We pray for peace and integrity
in all our dealings as individuals,
and in local, national and international conflicts;
for openness to hear God's wisdom
and courage to follow his lead.

Silence

Come, Holy Spirit:
guide our lives.

We pray for harmony and understanding
in our relationships with family and neighbours;
for the willingness both to give and to receive,
for the generosity of forgiving love.

Silence

Come, Holy Spirit:
guide our lives.

We pray for those whose weariness or pain
makes it difficult for them to pray;
may they sense the support and love
of the Church of God.

Silence

Come, Holy Spirit:
guide our lives.

We pray for those whose souls
have left behind their frail and broken bodies
to live in God's eternal company.
Bless and comfort their loved ones,
and bring us all in your good time,
to share the joy of heaven.

Silence

Come, Holy Spirit:
guide our lives.

We give you thanks for calling us by name
and keeping us safe
through all the storms and difficulties of this life,
in the power of the Holy Spirit.

Merciful Father,
**accept these prayers
for the sake of your Son,
our Saviour Jesus Christ. Amen.**

Breath of God

He breathed on them and said to them
'Receive the Holy Spirit'.
John 20:22

As the people of the living God,
let us join together in our prayers
for the Church and for the world.

Holy God, breathe your life into the Church;
breathe holiness and deepening faith,
breathe energy, inspired teaching and fervent praise;
unblock the channels and make us more receptive
to your gentleness and your power.

Silence

Breathe into us:
so that we live in you.

Holy God, breathe your life into the universe;
breathe responsible caring, honesty and compassion,
breathe right values and good stewardship,
peace and reconciliation, vision and hope.

Silence

Breathe into us:
so that we live in you.

Holy God, breathe your life
into our homes and places of work;
breathe increased patience and understanding,
and the courage to live the Christian life
when to do so brings ridicule or demands sacrifice.

Silence

Breathe into us:
so that we live in you.

Holy God, breathe your life into those who suffer;
breathe comfort and wholeness,
forgiveness and new confidence,
breathe peace of mind
and the knowledge of your love.

Silence

Breathe into us:
so that we live in you.

Holy God, breathe your life into the dead and dying;
breathe courage for the journey
and the realisation that you can be trusted.
Breathe life that lasts for ever.

Silence

Breathe into us:
so that we live in you.

Holy God, breathe your life into us now
as we offer you here our thanks and praise
for your life laid down out of love for us.
May our words be worked out
in fresh commitment to you.

Merciful Father,
accept these prayers
for the sake of your Son,
our Saviour Jesus Christ. Amen.

Set Our Hearts on Fire

He will baptise you with the Holy Spirit and fire.
Matthew 3:11

Let us pray to the God who has drawn us here today,
who loves us, and loves our world.

We pray that there may be a revival of longing
for your kingdom to come,
and a renewed commitment to working for it;
for a desire to live out our faith and worship
in our daily lives this week.

Silence

Come, Holy Spirit:
set our hearts on fire.

We pray that all who have authority and power
in our nation and our world may use it for good,
upholding and instigating what is right and fair,
and listening to the needs of those they represent.
May we recognise our responsibility
to support and stand up for God's values.

Silence

Come, Holy Spirit:
set our hearts on fire.

We pray that within our homes and communities
there may be a new awareness
of one another's gifts and needs,
more sensitivity and respect in our relationships;
may we reverence one another as fellow beings,
born of your creative love.

Silence

Come, Holy Spirit:
set our hearts on fire.

We pray for all who are oppressed,
downtrodden or despised;
we pray for those who will not eat today
and all who live in the degrading circumstances
of poverty and powerlessness;
we pray for a heart to put injustices right
and strive for a fair sharing of resources.

Silence

Come, Holy Spirit:
set our hearts on fire.

We pray for those whose life expectancy is short,
for the babies and children who have died
while we have been praying;
for all who have come to the end of their earthly life
and made that last journey through death;
thank you for your welcoming mercy
and the promise of eternal life.

Silence

Come, Holy Spirit:
set our hearts on fire.

We offer you our thanks and praise
for the scriptures that remind and inspire us,
and for your living Spirit which enables us.

Merciful Father,
accept these prayers
for the sake of your Son,
our Saviour Jesus Christ. Amen.

THE PEOPLE OF GOD

We Are Your People

I will be their God, and they shall be my people.
Jeremiah 31:33

Let us pray to the God who gives us so much
and loves us so completely.

We pray for a fresh outpouring of your Spirit
in all areas of the Church,
till our lives are so changed for good
that people notice and are drawn
to seek you for themselves.

Silence

We are your people:
and you are our God.

We pray for godly leaders and advisers
all over the world,
and for the courage to speak out
against injustice and evil.

Silence

We are your people:
and you are our God.

We pray for those affected
by our behaviour and our conversation,
that we may in future
encourage one another by all we say and do.

Silence

We are your people:
and you are our God.

We pray for those as yet unborn,
that the good news will reach them too;
we pray for those who have rejected God
because of the behaviour of his followers;
we pray for all who have lost their way.

Silence

We are your people:
and you are our God.

We pray for the dying,
especially those who are unprepared or frightened.
Welcome into your kingdom
those who have died in faith;
may they live with you for ever.

Silence

We are your people:
and you are our God.

Thank you, Lord, for the new life
you have enabled us to live.

Merciful Father,
accept these prayers
for the sake of your Son,
our Saviour Jesus Christ. Amen.

We Lift Our Hearts

Let us lift up our hearts as well as our hands
to God in heaven.
Lamentations 3:41

As we gather here in God's presence, let us pray.

We bring to you, Lord,
the Church in all its richness and all its need;
all its diversity and all its division.
Give us a fresh understanding
of what it means to live in you;
may all of us celebrate the reality
of your presence among us,
filling us with new life and new hope.

Silence

Lord, in your presence:
we lift our hearts to you.

We bring to you, Lord,
our nation, our world, our universe;
all the areas that are fastened shut to hold you out;
all the bewildered confusion
about who we are and why we are here;
all the doubts and insecurity,
and all the searching for inner peace.

Silence

Lord, in your presence:
we lift our hearts to you.

We bring to you, Lord, our homes and families,
and all the joys and sorrows of our relationships.

We bring the rooms in which we eat
and work and relax;
and invite you into them all.

Silence

Lord, in your presence:
we lift our hearts to you.

We bring to you, Lord,
those whom life has damaged,
and all who find it difficult to trust in you;
we bring you those who need refreshment and hope,
comfort, healing and inner serenity.

Silence

Lord, in your presence:
we lift our hearts to you.

We bring to you, Lord,
those who approach death with great fear
and those who die unprepared to meet you.
Have mercy on us all, forgive us all that is past
and gather us into your everlasting kingdom
of peace and joy.

Silence

Lord, in your presence:
we lift our hearts to you.

We bring to you, Lord, the love of our hearts
as we recall the extent of your love for us
which understands our frailty
and reaches out to us where we are.

Merciful Father,
**accept these prayers
for the sake of your Son,
our Saviour Jesus Christ. Amen.**

The Sheep of His Pasture

We are his people, and the sheep of his pasture.
Psalm 100:3

Let us humble ourselves in the presence of God
and pray to him for the Church and for the world.

Loving God, in all our ministry as the Church,
on Sundays and on weekdays,
may we give glory to you
and further your kingdom.
Direct us to those who are searching
and give us the wisdom to know
how best to draw them to your love.

Silence

We are your people:
the sheep of your pasture.

Loving God, may we actively seek to do good,
to stand up against injustice and work for peace;
Lord, rid the world of the terrible evils
that result from unvoiced objections,
and unspoken misgivings.
Give us the courage to act as true citizens of heaven.

Silence

We are your people:
the sheep of your pasture.

Loving God, may the ways we manage our homes,
decisions, time and money be in keeping with our calling

as inheritors of the kingdom.
May your love undergird all our loving.

Silence

We are your people:
the sheep of your pasture.

Loving God, search for the lost,
bring back those who have strayed,
bind up the injured, and strengthen the weak;
help us all to share in this work of loving care.

Silence

We are your people:
the sheep of your pasture.

Loving God, welcome into your kingdom
all whose lives show them to be your servants,
whether or not they have known you by name.
Prepare us all to meet you with the confidence
of sins confessed and forgiven.

Silence

We are your people:
the sheep of your pasture.

Loving God, you have shown us such love and humility;
we offer you our thanks and praise.

Merciful Father,
accept these prayers
for the sake of your Son,
our Saviour Jesus Christ. Amen.

At God's Invitation

When you said 'Come and worship me',
I answered, 'I will come, Lord'.
Psalm 27:8 (GNB)

Invited by our God, we have gathered here.
Let us now voice our prayers
for the Church and for the world.

Father, when either the traditional or the progressive
blinds us to the truth of your will,
clear our vision and speak through our prejudices
until we are once again open to your changing.
May we be, before anything else, your people,
sharing your concerns and desires.

Silence

At your invitation:
Lord, we come.

Father, we recognise how powerful
the influences are in our world
which distract many and lead away from your truth.
We pray for the quiet whisper of your wisdom
to be noticed and acknowledged in many lives;
we pray for widespread discipline of the heart,
a new openness to generosity of spirit.

Silence

At your invitation:
Lord, we come.

Father, may our homes and daily schedules
be part of the territory of your kingdom,

where it is your will which guides
and your love which rules.

Silence

At your invitation:
Lord, we come.

Father, our hearts rail against the cruelty
and unfairness of suffering and disease,
and we kneel now alongside all in pain
and weep with them, crying out to you
for comfort and the healing of your love.
For you are no bringer of evil to our lives,
but share our sorrow and give us the grace to bear it.

Silence

At your invitation:
Lord, we come.

Father, as death takes from us those we love
and we find it hard to live without them,
take from us all bitterness of heart and
let us share with them the peace you give,
over which death has no power at all.

Silence

At your invitation:
Lord, we come.

Father, it is such an honour
to be invited to your banquet;
make us worthy of our calling.

Merciful Father,
accept these prayers
for the sake of your Son,
our Saviour Jesus Christ. Amen.

Restore and Revive Us

Will you not revive us again?
Psalm 85:6

Let us quieten ourselves to notice our God,
here with us now,
and attentive to our deepest needs.

Lord, we long for our Church to be alive and active,
attentive to you,
and ready to go wherever you suggest.
Show us the work of the Church
from your point of view,
and develop our will to co-operate.

Silence

We call on your name, O God:
restore us and revive us.

Lord, we long for your kingdom
to come in our world,
and to flood with truth and love
the disillusion, hopelessness and terror
which traps the human spirit
and chokes its potential joy.

Silence

We call on your name, O God:
restore us and revive us.

Lord, come into the daily relationships
we so easily take for granted,
and enable us to value one another,

delighting in one another's richness,
and responding to one another's needs with love.

Silence

We call on your name, O God:
restore us and revive us.

Lord, you know the need and pain
of those we love and worry about.
As you look after them,
give them the sense of your caring presence
to uphold and sustain them.

Silence

We call on your name, O God:
restore us and revive us.

Lord, for us death can seem so cruel;
give us a better understanding of eternity,
and gather into your kingdom all those
whose earthly journey has come to an end.

Silence

We call on your name, O God:
restore us and revive us.

Thank you, Lord of hope,
for the way you surprise us with joy,
and show us the extraordinary and the wonderful
in the ordinary things of life.

Merciful Father,
accept these prayers
for the sake of your Son,
our Saviour Jesus Christ. Amen.

———————TRUST AND OBEY———————

Faith in God

Have faith in God.
Mark 11:22

Confident that God knows and loves each of us,
and understands our situation,
let us pray.

We pray for a deepening personal faith
in all Christians,
and renewed faith for all who are besieged by doubt.

Silence

You are our God:
in you we put our trust.

We pray that the Church
may be vigilant and courageous
in upholding the Christian faith,
and sensitive to the language and culture
of each person seeking for God in their lives.

Silence

You are our God:
in you we put our trust.

We long for a thirsting after God in our society;
for right living, justice and mercy
to be valued and worked for.

Silence

You are our God:
in you we put our trust.

We long for our homes and neighbourhoods
to reflect God's love
in our practical caring,
our hospitality and our parenting.

Silence

You are our God:
in you we put our trust.

We pray for those whose emotional pain
makes it difficult for them
to accept God's love and forgiveness;
and for all who feel that there is no hope.
We offer ourselves to be available
where you need us.

Silence

You are our God:
in you we put our trust.

We commend into your loving mercy the dying
and those who have made the journey through death.
With them we long to share the eternal joy
of your presence in heaven.

Silence

You are our God:
in you we put our trust.

We give you thanks and praise
for the endless love and patience you show us;
whenever we turn away,
please turn us back to you.

Merciful Father,
accept these prayers
for the sake of your Son,
our Saviour Jesus Christ. Amen.

All Things Work Together

We know that all things work together for good
for those who love God.
Romans 8:28

Let us attune our hearts to the God who loves us.

God of love,
we pray for all those who are newly baptised,
or who have recently found that you are real;
we pray for all in ordained and lay ministries,
and for those sensing a special calling.
Help us all to listen to your guiding.

Silence

In God:
all things work together for good.

God of power,
we pray for those who are in authority
and in positions of influence and responsibility;
may they be earthed in humility, courageous in integrity,
and mindful of the need to serve.

Silence

In God:
all things work together for good.

God of mercy,
we call to mind those with whom we share
the work and leisure of our life;
we pray for those we treasure and those we battle with,
and ask you to breathe into all our relationships
the forgiving love which cleanses and heals.

Silence

In God:
all things work together for good.

God of wholeness,
we remember those who are aching today
in body, mind or spirit;
knowing that nothing is unredeemable,
we ask that you will bring good
even out of these barren places.

Silence

In God:
all things work together for good.

God of life,
we pray for those whose earthly lives have ended;
we remember those who have died
violently and tragically, suddenly and unprepared.
We give you thanks for lives well lived
and for happy memories.
May they rest in the eternal peace of heaven.

Silence

In God:
all things work together for good.

God of faithfulness,
we thank you for the way
you always keep your promises
and never let us down.

Merciful Father,
accept these prayers
for the sake of your Son,
our Saviour Jesus Christ. Amen.

We Shall Not Want

The Lord is my shepherd, I shall not want.
Psalm 23:1

Let us pray to God our Father,
knowing that we are all precious to him.

Father, we thank you for all those
who give to support the work of the Church;
bless our giving, guide our spending,
and help us to value the true wealth
of your abundant love.

Silence

The Lord is our shepherd:
there is nothing we shall want.

We pray for the world's economy;
for fair management and distribution of resources;
for fair trade and just wages;
for greater awareness and concern about injustice;
for a commitment to our responsibilities
as planet-sharers and earth-dwellers.

Silence

The Lord is our shepherd:
there is nothing we shall want.

We pray for all parents with young children,
thanking you for them
and asking you to bless and guide their parenting;
we pray for families in debt;
for those whose homes have been repossessed,

and those whose financial security
makes them forgetful of your love.

Silence

The Lord is our shepherd:
there is nothing we shall want.

We pray for those who are burdened
with financial worries
and all who struggle to make ends meet,
all over the world;
we pray for the emotionally and spiritually bankrupt,
and those who do not yet know God's love for them.

Silence

The Lord is our shepherd:
there is nothing we shall want.

We pray for those who have died,
and those on that last journey at this moment;
for a merciful judgement
and the everlasting joy of heaven.

Silence

The Lord is our shepherd:
there is nothing we shall want.

Father, we give you thanks
for the extraordinary generosity of your love for us,
which lasts beyond death into the whole of eternity.

Merciful Father,
accept these prayers
for the sake of your Son,
our Saviour Jesus Christ. Amen.

Deliver Us from Evil

I ask you to protect them from the evil one.
John 17:15

As children of our heavenly Father,
who knows us so well and loves us completely,
let us pray.

Father, knowing our weakness in the face of temptation,
we ask for your strength and protection
so that, though we stumble,
we shall not fall headlong.

Silence　　　　　　　　Lead us not into temptation:
but deliver us from evil.

Father, we pray for all those who are fighting temptation
and finding it difficult to resist.
We ask you to help them see clearly,
and equip them with all they need
to choose what is right.

Silence　　　　　　　　Lead us not into temptation:
but deliver us from evil.

Father, we pray for the Church
as it struggles to steer a straight course
true to your calling.
We pray for wisdom and courage,
honesty and the willingness to be vulnerable.

Silence　　　　　　　　Lead us not into temptation:
but deliver us from evil.

Father, we pray for those we love,
whose company we enjoy.
We pray too for those who irritate us
and those whom we annoy.

Silence   Lead us not into temptation:
                                       but deliver us from evil.

Father, we stand alongside all those who suffer,
all whose lives are in chaos or despair,
and all who live in the dark prison of guilt.
We pray for your reassurance and peace,
your understanding and compassion.

Silence   Lead us not into temptation:
                                       but deliver us from evil.

We pray for the dying,
especially the unnoticed and despised.
We pray for those who have gone through death
and now see you face to face,
that they may receive your merciful forgiveness
and know the joy of living with you for ever.

Silence   Lead us not into temptation:
                                       but deliver us from evil.

Father, we thank you for the knowledge
that nothing is beyond your forgiveness,
and no one beyond the limits of your love.

Silence

Merciful Father
**accept these prayers
for the sake of your Son,
our Saviour Jesus Christ. Amen.**

The Service of God

Do not lag in zeal, be ardent in spirit, serve the Lord.
Romans 12:11

God has chosen to call us here
and we have chosen to come.
Let us pray to him now.

Lord, we want to pray for stronger faith
and the courage to live up to our calling;
for the grace to act always
with the generosity of spirit you show to us,
until the whole Church models the wisdom
which the world counts as foolishness.

Silence

Holy God:
we commit ourselves to your service.

Lord, we want to pray
about all the unresolved conflicts in our world.
We ask you to give us your desire for peace,
your spirit of discernment,
your understanding of unspoken needs,
and your capacity for forgiveness.

Silence

Holy God:
we commit ourselves to your service.

Lord, we want to pray
for the homes and families we represent,
and for all with whom we live and work.
Help us to recognise the opportunities

for generous, loving service
and take away any destructive possessiveness
or self-interest.

Silence

Holy God:
we commit ourselves to your service.

Lord, we pray for peace of mind and spirit
in all those who are distressed or enveloped in pain.
May they know the reality of your inner healing,
and may even the worst situations
become places of growth and new life.

Silence

Holy God:
we commit ourselves to your service.

Lord, we pray for those approaching death
with fear, resentment and anger,
and for all who counsel the dying and the bereaved.
We pray that those who have died will know
the joy of everlasting life with you.

Silence

Holy God:
we commit ourselves to your service.

Lord, we thank you
for the extraordinary generosity of your love,
which takes us by surprise and refreshes us,
and which always appears
where we least think to look for it.

Merciful Father,
**accept these prayers
for the sake of your Son,
our Saviour Jesus Christ. Amen.**

Send Me

And I said 'Here am I; send me!'
Isaiah 6:8

Let us gather with our prayers
before the God who knows each of us by name.

Father, we thank you that your Church
is made up of real people,
that it is a school for sinners,
and that you can work with us and through us
straight away.

Silence

Here I am, Lord:
send me!

Father, we pray for the newly baptised
and those who have recently returned to you;
help us, as your Church, to support them well
and delight in them as members together
of the body of Christ.

Silence

Here I am, Lord:
send me!

Father, we pray for your strength and protection
against all hypocrisy and double standards
in our society.
We pray for a spirit of genuine service
among all who lead and in all areas
where we have authority.

Silence

Here I am, Lord:
send me!

Father, we pray that you will make
our homes and our relationships
places where people know,
by the way we look at them and treat them,
that they are valued, cherished
and respected for who they are.

Silence

Here I am, Lord:
send me!

Father, as we call to mind all who have learned
to regard themselves with contempt,
draw near to them and whisper their true name
so that they discern the truth
of your love and respect for them.
And use our lives to affirm one another.

Silence

Here I am, Lord:
send me!

We pray for the dying
and those who have recently died,
commending them to the joy
and safe-keeping of your love.
We give thanks for all those who know and love us
and help us grow in faith.

Merciful Father,
**accept these prayers
for the sake of your Son,
our Saviour Jesus Christ. Amen.**

SPECIAL DAYS AND SEASONS

Advent

The night is far gone, the day is near.
Romans 13:12

Let us pray to the God of all time and space,
in whose love we exist
and by whose love we are saved.

As we prepare ourselves
for the time when Christ comes again in glory,
we pray for the grace and honesty
to see what needs transforming in our lives as individuals
and as members of the Church of God.

Silence

O come:
let us walk in the light of the Lord.

May all church leaders, pastors and teachers be directed,
inspired and upheld by the living Spirit of God,
and may there be a deepening
of love and commitment in all Christians the world over.

Silence

O come:
let us walk in the light of the Lord.

May the leaders of this nation and of all the nations
be drawn increasingly to understand
God's ways of justice and righteousness,
and be filled with the longing
to do what is right and honest and good.

Silence

O come:
let us walk in the light of the Lord.

May all the families on earth be blessed with mutual love
and caring consideration one of another;
may arguments and misunderstandings
be properly resolved,
and difficult relationships refreshed and healed.

Silence

O come:
let us walk in the light of the Lord.

May those for whom the days and nights
creep past in pain or sorrow be given comfort and hope;
may the frightened find reassurance
and the anxious find peace of mind.

Silence

O come:
let us walk in the light of the Lord.

May those who have reached the point of death
be given the knowledge of God's closeness
on that last journey;
and may those who have died
know the eternal peace and joy of heaven.

Silence

O come:
let us walk in the light of the Lord.

May we all be given a new enthusiasm
for walking God's way, clothed in the armour of light.

Merciful Father,
**accept these prayers
for the sake of your Son,
our Saviour Jesus Christ. Amen.**

Epiphany

The light shines in the darkness,
and the darkness did not overcome it.
John 1:5

We are all companions on a spiritual journey.
As we travel together, let us pray.

Silence

Light of the world:
shine in our darkness.

We pray that the worldwide Church
may always be ready
to travel in your way
and in your direction.

Silence

Light of the world:
shine in our darkness.

We pray for the nations
as they live through conflicts
and struggle with identity.
We long for all peoples
to acknowledge the true and living God.

Silence

Light of the world:
shine in our darkness.

We pray for the families and the streets we represent,
asking for a spirit of generous love,
understanding and mutual respect.

Silence

Light of the world:
shine in our darkness.

We pray for all who are finding their way
tedious, lonely or frightening at the moment;
for those who have lost their way
and do not know what to do for the best.

Silence

Light of the world:
shine in our darkness.

We pray for those who have come
to the end of their earthly journey,
and for those who have died unprepared.

Silence

Light of the world:
shine in our darkness.

We offer our thanks and praise
for the way you see us when we are still far off
and welcome us home.

Merciful Father,
**accept these prayers
for the sake of your Son,
our Saviour Jesus Christ. Amen.**

Mothering Sunday

I was to them like those who lift infants to their cheeks.
Hosea 11:4

Let us pray to our loving parent God,
as children in one family.

We thank you, loving God,
for giving us one another to enjoy,
to laugh and cry with, to learn to live with.
May even our conflicts and arguments be used
in helping us to grow up in your love.

Silence

Loving God:
we give you thanks.

Thank you, loving God, for showing us the way to love
and giving us opportunities to give,
to take second place, to accept people as they are,
to forgive them when they annoy us,
and look for their needs before our own.

Silence

Loving God:
we give you thanks.

Thank you, loving God, for the world we live in,
for the colours and shapes, the sounds and textures in it.
Thank you for giving us minds and emotions
and help us to reverence the whole of creation.

Silence

Loving God:
we give you thanks.

Thank you, loving God, for comfort and sympathy,
reassurance and practical caring when we are ill or sad.
Make us all more aware of the needs of those around us
and let our loving show in action.

Silence

Loving God:
we give you thanks.

Thank you, loving God,
for your promise to be with us always,
and not just until we die.
We remember with affection
those of our parents who loved us into existence
and now live in eternity.
Gather up into your loving arms
those who have recently died
and comfort all whose memories
make them aware of loss today.

Silence

Loving God:
we give you thanks.

Thank you, loving God, for giving us space and support,
guidance and forgiveness, challenge and reassurance.

Merciful Father,
accept these prayers
for the sake of your Son,
our Saviour Jesus Christ. Amen.

Ascension Day

He raised him from the dead and seated him at his
right hand in the heavenly places.
Ephesians 1:20

As we celebrate together, let us pray together.

God of love, as we celebrate this festival
of Jesus' entry into heaven as Saviour and Lord,
we pray for unity in the Church
and reconciliation and renewed vision.

Silence

Both heaven and earth:
are full of God's glory.

As we recall the shout of praise in heaven
as the Lamb of God appears,
we pray for all who are hailed as heroes
and given great honour on earth;
for all who worship anyone or anything
other than the true God.

Silence

Both heaven and earth:
are full of God's glory.

We pray for all farewells and homecomings
among our families and in our community,
and for all who have lost touch with loved ones
and long for reunion.

Silence

Both heaven and earth:
are full of God's glory.

We pray for those who are full of tears,
and cannot imagine being happy again;
we pray for the hardened and callous,
whose inner hurts have never yet been healed.
We pray for wholeness and comfort and new life.

Silence

Both heaven and earth:
are full of God's glory.

We commend to your eternal love
those we remember who have died,
and we pray too for those
who miss their physical presence.

Silence

Both heaven and earth:
are full of God's glory.

We praise and bless you, God our maker,
for the way you draw us deeper
into the meaning of life.

Merciful Father,
accept these prayers
for the sake of your Son,
our Saviour Jesus Christ. Amen.

Trinity Sunday

The grace of the Lord Jesus Christ, the love of God,
and the communion of the Holy Spirit be with all of you.
2 Corinthians 13:13

Let us pray to the Father,
in the power of the Holy Spirit,
through Jesus, the Son.

We pray for all theologians
and those who teach the faith
in colleges and Bible study groups
throughout the Church.
We pray for godly wisdom and human insight.

Silence

Holy God:
help us to know you more.

We pray for peace and co-operation,
harmony and mutual respect
in all our dealings with one another
locally, nationally and internationally.

Silence

Holy God:
help us to know you more.

We pray for those who depend on us,
and those on whom we depend,
for our physical and spiritual needs.
Enable us to honour one another
as children of one Father.

Silence

Holy God:
help us to know you more.

We pray for those who feel fragmented;
and for those forced to live apart from loved ones
through war, political unrest,
natural disasters or poverty.
We commend their pain to your comforting.

Silence

Holy God:
help us to know you more.

We remember those who told us of you
through their words and lives;
we think of those who have died in faith
and ask that we may share with them
in the joy of your presence for ever.

Silence

Holy God:
help us to know you more.

We give you thanks for meeting us where we are,
and travelling with us in person.

Merciful Father,
**accept these prayers
for the sake of your Son,
our Saviour Jesus Christ. Amen.**

INDEXES

Topical Index

THE CHURCH

THE WORLD

N.B. Each set of prayers includes intercessions for the dying or those who have died.

Biblical Index